PUFFIN

KNOW-IT-A

MIGHTY EGYPTIANS

If being a writer wasn't Nigel Crowle's full-time job,
he'd still be doing it for fun. He's written for
children's TV series like *Tweenies*, *The Chuckle
Brothers* and *Balamory*, and for big stars like
Ant and Dec, Elton John, Lenny Henry,
Caroline Quentin, Donny Osmond,
Basil Brush and Jonathan Ross.
He lives in Cardiff with his wife, son and
dog where his scripts, plays and books
hopefully keep his family:
(a) occupied
(b) amused
(c) in the manner to which they've
become accustomed (especially Dexter Dog).

KNOW-IT-ALL GUIDES

MIGHTY EGYPTIANS

FAR-OUT FACTS to impress your FRIENDS!

Nigel Crowle

Illustrated by Martin Chatterton

PUFFIN BOOKS

Published by the Penguin Group
Penguin Books Ltd, 80 Strand, London WC2R 0RL, England
Penguin Group (USA) Inc., 375 Hudson Street, New York, New York 10014, USA
Penguin Group (Canada), 90 Eglinton Avenue East, Suite 700, Toronto, Ontario,
Canada M4P 2Y3 (a division of Pearson Penguin Canada Inc.)
Penguin Ireland, 25 St Stephen's Green, Dublin 2, Ireland
(a division of Penguin Books Ltd)
Penguin Group (Australia), 250 Camberwell Road, Camberwell, Victoria 3124, Australia
(a division of Pearson Australia Group Pty Ltd)
Penguin Books India Pvt Ltd, 11 Community Centre, Panchsheel Park,
New Delhi – 110 017, India
Penguin Group (NZ), 67 Apollo Drive, Mairangi Bay, Auckland 1310, New Zealand
(a division of Pearson New Zealand Ltd)
Penguin Books (South Africa) (Pty) Ltd, 24 Sturdee Avenue, Rosebank,
Johannesburg 2196, South Africa

Penguin Books Ltd, Registered Offices: 80 Strand, London WC2R 0RL, England

penguin.com

Published 2007
1

Text copyright © Nigel Crowle, 2007
Illustrations copyright © Martin Chatterton, 2007
Designed by Tony Fleetwood
All rights reserved

The moral right of the author and illustrator has been asserted

Set in Bookman Old Style
Made and printed in England by Clays Ltd, St Ives plc

                         h Library Cataloguing i   Publication Data
                         for this book is av   lable from the British Library

                         ISBN: 978-0-141-   073–1

The Great Pyramids were built as a monument to the mighty Egyptian god-kings. In a slightly different way, I'd like these books to stand as a monument to the support of my equally mighty family and friends.

A thousand thanks to those rulers of the Crowle dynasty: my wife, Melanie, my very own Cleopatra, and my son, Siôn, the Boy King. They both laugh royally, on a daily basis, at (almost) all of my ancient jokes. The ancient Egyptians worshipped their animals, so it seems appropriate to mention the fourth member of our family: Dexter the Dog. He encourages me too, with big licks and tail wags!

I also have to thank my own Mummy – not the Egyptian kind! – and Daddy: Joan and Ken Crowle, who have encouraged me for centuries . . . well, all my life, at least!

My friend Emma Twomlow always enjoys reading my books so I hope she likes this one. (I also hope she likes seeing her name!)

Thanks to Trish Paterson for lending me her brilliant reference book. Thanks also to my editor, Jane Richardson, who is ever-helpful (and always right!) when it comes to deciding what facts go into a book like this. Oh, and I mustn't forget my agent Sarah Manson. Finally, many thanks to Martin Chatterton for all his fantastic illustrations – Egyptian and otherwise.

Don't forget to flick the top right-hand corner of every page and see the pyramid take off!

Check out more fab facts at
know-it-all-guides.co.uk

Contents

So, You Want to Know About . . . Mighty Egyptians?

All right – picture the scene. You're scrabbling around the Egyptian sands and you find the entrance to an ancient Egyptian tomb. Carefully, you scratch away the sands and stones and you wriggle along the narrow entrance tunnel to an underground burial chamber. In front of you, glittering in the light of your torch, is a beautiful sarcophagus.

Sweating heavily, you ease the lid open, straining to see the secrets that have lain, undisturbed for thousands of years.

You gulp nervously as you realize that you are actually looking at . . . the Know-it-All Guide to Mighty Egyptians! You marvel at the knowledge this book gives you – you'll no doubt use it to impress both your friends and your family.

Journey back in time to discover everything you never knew you never knew about the secrets of a civilization that began along the banks of the River Nile.

But be warned – every so often you'll find a fact that is complete tosh. An out-and-out lie. An outrageous falsehood. A load of balderdash, in fact! So, that's your challenge – can you Find That Fib?

Map of Modern Egypt

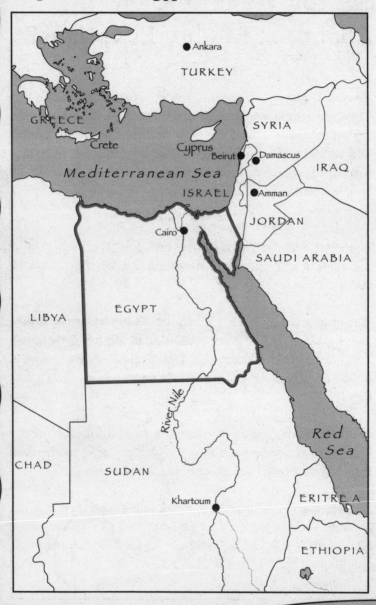

Map of the Egyptian Empire 1500–1300BC (New Kingdom)

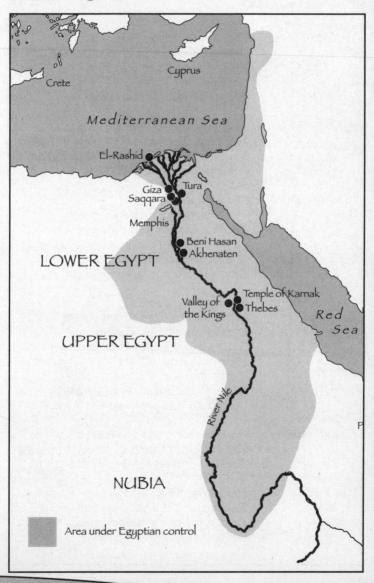

Crete

Cyprus

Mediterranean Sea

El-Rashid

Giza · Tura
Saqqara

Memphis

Beni Hasan
Akhenaten

LOWER EGYPT

Temple of Karnak
Valley of
the Kings · Thebes

*Red
Sea*

UPPER EGYPT

River Nile

NUBIA

Area under Egyptian control

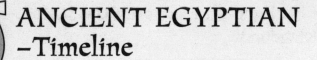

ANCIENT EGYPTIAN
–Timeline

3100–2950 BC   *Late Predynastic Period*
Unification of Upper and Lower Egypt
Early kings buried in royal tombs at
Abydos
Hieroglyphics first appear

2950–2686 BC   *Early Dynastic Period*
The capital city of Memphis is founded
The first pyramid – the Step Pyramid
– is built at Saqqara

2686–2181 BC   *Old Kingdom*
The Great Pyramids are built
Trade expands the empire

2181–1975 BC   *First Intermediate Period*
Egypt divides into two states

1975–1700 BC   *Middle Kingdom*
Mentuhotep II reunites Egypt
Capital moves to Thebes
Amenemhat I moves capital back to
Memphis and builds a new palace
Egypt conquers Lower Nubia
Many works of classic art and
literature are produced

1700–1550 BC   *Second Intermediate Period*
The north is taken over by the Hyksos
Theban dynasty rules in the south

1550–1075 BC   *New Kingdom*
Thutmose I military campaign in Near
East and Africa helps build
Egyptian Empire

Splendid tombs built in Valley of the Kings
The first woman pharaoh, Hatshepsut, reigned 1498–1483 BC
Akhenaten reigned 1353–1336 BC
Building of Temple at Luxor, 1380 BC
Reign of young pharaoh Tutankhamun, 1336–1327 BC
Rameses III reigned 1183–1152 BC

1075–715 BC   *Third Intermediate Period*
Libyans and then Nubians invade Egypt

715–332 BC   *Late Period*
Assyrians conquer Egypt for a while then Persians conquer Egypt in 525 BC
Egypt gains independence (404–343 BC)

332 BC–AD 395   *Greco-Roman Period*
Alexander the Great occupies Egypt (332 BC) and Alexandria becomes the capital. Alexander's general Ptolemy becomes pharaoh. Founds an important dynasty (305 BC)
Rosetta Stone inscribed
Reign of Cleopatra VII, 51–30 BC
Rome conquers Egypt and it becomes a part of the Roman Empire (30 BC)
Last known use of hieroglyphics

Note – *the dates are approximate. Even historians are not sure of the exact dates for the beginning and ends of the periods.*

Hieroglyphic Alphabet

Here are some of the real symbols which the ancient Egyptians used in writing their alphabet. There's a space next to each sign for you to have a go at drawing it.

Hieroglyphics are usually written from left to right, but they also appear from right to left. The general rule is the heads of the animal characters should face the opposite direction to which you read. So if the heads are facing left, you should read from left to right.

a eagle - - - - - - -

a arm - - - - - - -

b leg - - - - - - -

ch tether - - - - - - -

c basket - - - - - - -

d hand - - - - - - -

ee two reeds - - - - - - -

f viper - - - - - - -

g jar stand - - - - - - -

h house - - - - - - -

i reed - - - - - - -

j cobra - - - - - - -

k basket -------		**s** bolt -------
l lion -------		**ss** cloth -------
m owl -------		**sh** pool -------
n water -------		**t** bread -------
o lasso -------		**u** rope -------
oo chick -------		**v** viper -------
p door -------		**w** chick -------
q slope -------		**y** reeds -------
r mouth -------		**z** bolt -------

The ancient Egyptians also had symbols for numbers. For example ∩ was the unit used for number 10. If you wanted to write the number 30, you had to write the ∩ symbol three times – gettit? And so you counted upwards in units of ten. One other unit was |, which was used for number 1. You might find that useful too.

So, if you wanted to write the number 33, you had to write that ∩ symbol three times, and then write | three times, as well.

Ancient Egyptian Numerals

I	II	III	II II	III II	III III	III III	IIII IIII	III III III
1	**2**	**3**	**4**	**5**	**6**	**7**	**8**	**9**

∩	ℓ		⚱	𓆏	𓁨
10	**100**	**1000**	**10,000**	**100,000**	**1,000,000**

Take a look at the hieroglyphic alphabet, and work out which letters – and numbers – mean the same as our modern alphabet. With a bit of practice, you'll be able to work out the following secret message!

1. Life in Ancient Egypt

Before you dive in, remember each chapter does contain a completely made-up story among all the facts. It's up to you to spot it . . . and then check you were right by flipping to the end of this book. Good luck as you try to Find That Fib!

It's unlikely that the great civilization of Egypt would exist without its unusual geography. The mighty River Nile is the longest in the world, and it flows through a valley in the Egyptian desert. The narrow, fertile strips of land either side of the river allowed settlements, towns and cities to be built along the 6,695-kilometre strip, as the soil was perfect for growing crops and tending animals. In fact, there was so much fertile land that farmers could even spare some to grow flowers, which were used as decorations, offerings to the gods and to make perfume. The River Nile was also an important method of transport, as it enabled easy transport throughout the kingdom.

The ancient Egyptians thought of Egypt as being divided into two types of land – the 'blue land' and the 'pink land'. The 'blue land' was the name given to the land that had been stained by the bright blue pollen dropping from a type of reed that only grows on the steeper banks of the Nile. The 'pink land' was the area surrounding the Nile, which was covered with flamingos before it was turned over to farmland.

How to Live Life in Ancient Egypt

1. If you were rich, life was good and you enjoyed your luxuries.
2. If you were poor, you earned your daily bread by working as a labourer – freedom was limited, but you could still own land.
3. If you were a skilled worker, you were rewarded for being clever at your craft, and you lived with your fellow craftsmen in a separate part of a town.

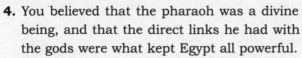

4. You believed that the pharaoh was a divine being, and that the direct links he had with the gods were what kept Egypt all powerful.

5. You probably didn't keep slaves, which were rare in Egypt and were almost always foreign captives who were even allowed to own property.

Egyptian workers lived in houses built in cramped villages with narrow streets near their workplaces, tomb sites or farmlands. Their houses were made of mud bricks mixed with straw and dried in the sun. These buildings weren't terribly sturdy and when one mud house fell to pieces another one was simply built on top of the crumbled mud.

Posh Egyptians lived in houses on comfortable estates, outside the towns. Even though their houses were well built, with high ceilings, swimming pools and servants' quarters, they had surprisingly little furniture. Only the really wealthy had chairs, but leather cushions on top of stools were comfy enough for most of the well-off . . .

Quickie Quiz

In a typical city (like Tell el Daba in the Nile Delta) at what age did the average ancient Egyptian male die? Was it:

a) twenty?
b) sixty-six?
c) thirty-four?

The answer's c). Ancient Egyptian men lived on average until they were thirty-four years old.

Bad news for ancient Egyptian women, though – due to childbirth problems, they tended to die when they were only thirty years of age. Which is probably why family life was highly valued in Egyptian culture and children were regarded as a blessing.

Though a husband's word was law, and his wife had to care for his every need in the home, **Egyptian women** had **rights and privileges**, which was unusual for the time. Unlike other civilizations, women were allowed to run a business, own pieces of land and give evidence in a court of law.

The Name Game

Common names in ancient Egypt were nouns or adjectives, such as 'Neferet', which means 'beautiful woman'. The female form of names often ended in 'et'. Other names were made up of phrases such as 'Rahotep', meaning 'Ra is satisfied'.

Newborn babies were given a name at birth, which was written down together with any nicknames, the father's name, sometimes the mother's name, and the father's job, rank or position in Egyptian society. This led to some children having an awful lot of names!

In Thebes, many middle-class Egyptians named their children 'Taueret' after the goddess of childbirth. Taueret was more animal-like than you'd expect.

Four Ways in which Taueret was Imagined by Ancient Egyptians

1. As a hippo standing upright.
2. As a hippo with the paws and mane of a lion.
3. As a hippo with a crocodile's tail.
4. As a hippo with a cow's horns.

Quickie Quiz

Which of these were very popular Egyptian names? Were they:

a) **Khenemet, Hotep, Ankh?**
b) **Ryan, Tom, Grant?**
c) **Dexter, Otis, Rover?**

The answer's a). Words or phrases were often used in Egyptian names. These included: 'Khenemet', which meant 'one who is joined with'; 'Hotep', which meant 'peace'; and 'Ankh', the word for 'life'.

Growing up in Ancient Egypt

Top Four Ancient Egyptian Childhood Toys
1. Wooden pull-along toy crocodiles and horses.
2. Balls made from rags.
3. Rattles.
4. Spinning tops made of stone.

Only the sons of scribes or noblemen went to **school** at the local temple, where they were taught reading, writing and mathematics. Sometimes their sisters were lucky enough to go to school too. But mostly Egyptian children grew up **learning a trade** from their parents. Boys as young as four were taught to do the same jobs as their fathers, while girls were taught household tasks like cooking, spinning and weaving.

2. Death and Mummification

Pharaohs were thought of as gods and so, when they died, they were preserved in tombs as mummies. By honouring the nobility in this way, ordinary Egyptians believed that everyday life would continue smoothly. Show how smooth you can be when you Find That Fib!

When a person died, everything a dead person had needed in life was **placed in the tomb** with him or her. This included furniture, clothes and also small statues made of stone or glazed pottery. This was because the Egyptians believed in life after death and these statues would help the deceased in the afterlife.

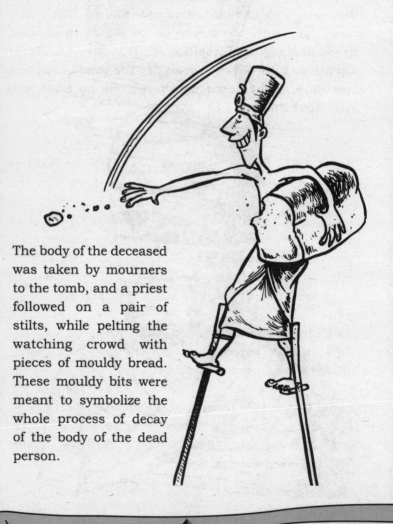

The body of the deceased was taken by mourners to the tomb, and a priest followed on a pair of stilts, while pelting the watching crowd with pieces of mouldy bread. These mouldy bits were meant to symbolize the whole process of decay of the body of the dead person.

During the funeral, priests read spells from the **_Book of the Dead_** to ease the journey into the afterlife for the dead person. This book was a collection of magic spells, formulae, passwords and directions written for the dead person as they made their way into the Underworld. Apart from acting as a kind of Death Passport, identifying them as they made their final journey, it also gave them the protection of the gods.

Differences Between 'Ba' and 'Ka'
'Ba' – a dead person's personality
'Ka' – a dead person's spirit

The Ba supposedly hovered above the mummified body like a bird and helped the dead person's body rejoin its Ka. Once it had found its spirit again, the dead person could live on in the next world.

Things to Do in Ancient Egypt when You're Dead

1. Make sure that good luck symbols or small objects called 'talismans' have been placed on your mummified body.

2. Use the passwords written in the Book of the Dead to help your body find safe passage as you leave the Land of the Living and enter the Kingdom of the Dead.

3. Say hello to either the god Anubis or Horus who would show you the way to the sovereign judge, Osiris. (For more on these gods, see page 71.)

4. Kiss the door frame as you enter the vast Hall Of Double Justice.

5. Notice Maat, goddess of truth and justice, standing behind a set of large weighing scales in the centre of the hall. Notice also that Maat has placed your heart on the scales, ready to weigh it against a feather, which is the symbol of truth.

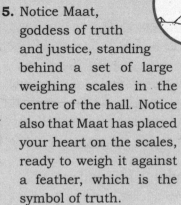

6. Dodge Ammit 'the Devourer' – a mixed-up monster that's part lion, part hippo and part crocodile and is licking its lips to eat the hearts of the guilty.

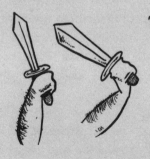

7. Examine your conscience – say what good you've done, and what bad you've done – in front of fourteen judges holding sharp swords (that's one judge for each province of Egypt).

8. Tell the judges in turn that you're free from sin.

9. Hope that your heart balances perfectly. Otherwise your heart will be devoured by Ammit.

If the scales balanced, then Osiris would look well upon you and say, 'Let the deceased depart victorious. Let him go wherever he wishes to mingle freely with the gods and the spirits of the dead.' Not a bad message from a god who looks like a mummified man, with decaying flesh held in place by flapping bandages.

From then on, you'd still be dead but at least you'd lead a life of happiness in the kingdom of Osiris.

Making Mummies

Getting made into a mummy took about **seventy days** and was a **very expensive** process. That's why mummies were generally only made of pharaohs, nobles or rich people.

Hairdressers and beauty experts would do their best to make a dead body look as lifelike as possible – so they could carry on using their body in their life after death.

However, the mummified bodies of many ordinary Egyptians have also been found. They'd been buried in **desert sand hollows**, which mummified them naturally. Any body fluids that might rot human flesh would be dried up or drained away by the hot sands. This heat would dry out the bodies and preserve skin, hair and nails.

The first real mummies emerged around **3000 BC**. They were **wrapped in linen** dipped in plaster and resin to make sure it held a body's shape, using up to 375 metres' worth of material. But the mummies quickly rotted away into a horrible, disgusting gooey mess. However, by about **2600 BC**, the Egyptians realized that the bodies wouldn't putrefy if they **removed the soft organs** of the body before wrapping.

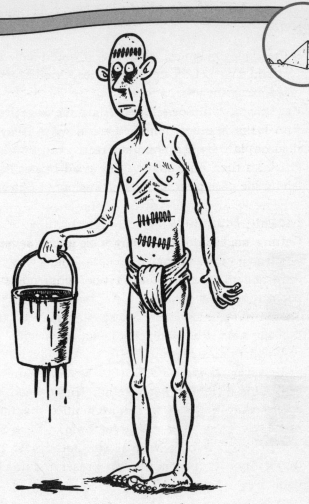

Don't read this next part about Making A Mummy if you've just eaten!

The **stomach**, **intestines**, the **brains** and other **internal organs** were taken out. However, the heart was always left in the body, as the Egyptians thought the **heart a was the key to a person's character**. Afterwards, the hollow body was dried out with salts and the skin was rubbed with oils.

Three Ways to Remove Someone's Brains before Mummification

1. Stick a bronze needle with a hook or spiral on the end up a nostril. Enter the base of the skull at the root of the nose. Twiddle around until bits of brain have been pulled down through the nasal passage. (Only use this method if you are skilful with a needle and have a steady hand . . .)

2. Pop out an eye. Break through the upper wall of the eye socket. Reveal a larger opening for extracting the brain.

3. Chop off the head. Use a spoon to take out the brain through the passage at the back of the skull. Put the head on a stick and place it back on the body and hold it in place with bandages.

Quickie Quiz

Where did Egyptians store the squishy bits they removed from people's dead bodies before they were embalmed and turned into mummies? Was it:

a) in their pockets?

b) on a bedside table?

c) in special jars?

The answer's c). Vital organs had to be removed from bodies before they were embalmed. These body parts were placed in canopic vases or jugs (which some people have called canopic jars). They were then looked after by a combination of goddesses and guards.

Body Part	Goddess Protector	Guard (one of four sons of Horus)
Intestine	Scorpion-goddess Serket	Hawk-headed Qebehsenuf
Liver	Isis	Human-headed Imset
Lungs	Nephthys	Baboon-headed Happy
Stomach	Neith	Jackal-headed Duamutef

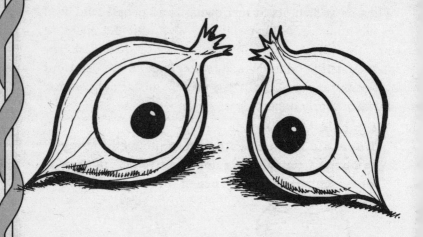

An **embalmer** – someone who preserved a dead body – would **replace the eyes** of a mummy (such as Rameses III) with scraps of cloth rolled into balls and dotted with black paint. Another method (as used upon Rameses IV) used two little onions with eyeballs painted on them and placed inside the mummy's empty eye sockets.

Some of the Ingredients Used in Embalming Fluid to Preserve Dead Bodies

Cedar oil

Liquid oil of gebety

Cummin oil

Oil from Lebanon

Wax

Rubber

Turpentine

Sweet-smelling incense

Natron (a type of salt)

When a cat died, its former owners and people who lived in the house would get really, really upset. So upset, in fact, that they'd shave their eyebrows to show just how stricken with grief they really were. Then they'd carry out the elaborate and expensive process of mummification on their dearly departed pet.

Seven Steps to Mummify a Cat

(Unless your mummifying skills are up to scratch, don't attempt this on your own cat!)

1. Remove all internal organs.
2. Stuff body of cat with sand or packing material.
3. Place cat in a sitting position.
4. Wrap cat's body tightly in linen.
5. Use black ink to paint faces and designs on wrapped body of cat.
6. Don't use chemicals – let cat dry out naturally.
7. Place a bowl of milk on the tomb floor, along with mice and rats for the cat to eat in the afterlife!

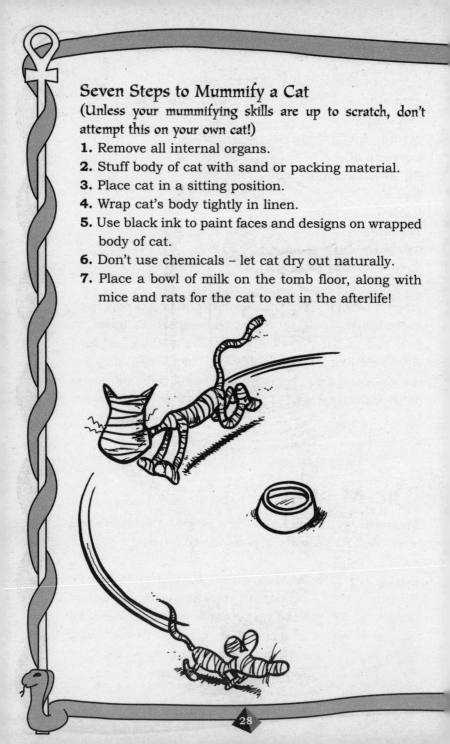

On the label: Dosage: 2 measures twice a day

The Mummy Trade

Mummies were believed to be a powerful medicine and were used for all sorts of potions and lotions.

During the **Middle Ages**, it was common practice for doctors to tell ailing patients that they should swallow 'bitumen', or **ground-up mummies**, as a cure for various kinds of diseases. This resulted in a thriving trade in whole dead mummies being transported from Egypt to Europe throughout the Dark Ages.

During the **sixteenth century**, it became the fashion to use **bits of Egyptian mummies** to cure ailments. If you had a bruise, you rubbed a piece of a mummy on it. If you had tummy pains, you actually . . . gulp . . . swallowed bits of the mummies themselves! Yuckkkk! People stopped this disgusting treatment during the seventeenth century – but only because Egyptian governors added a tax on all mummy traders, which made it impossible to make money out of the practice . . .

By the **nineteenth century**, the mummy trade was booming as explorers came home from archaeological trips to Egypt laden down with real mummies and other treasures. Then they showed off their souvenirs at lavish parties where the highlight was a bizarre version of 'Pass the Parcel' in which the **mummy was unwrapped** in all its gory glory, in front of the partygoers. Now, there's a sight to put you off your jelly and blancmange, eh?

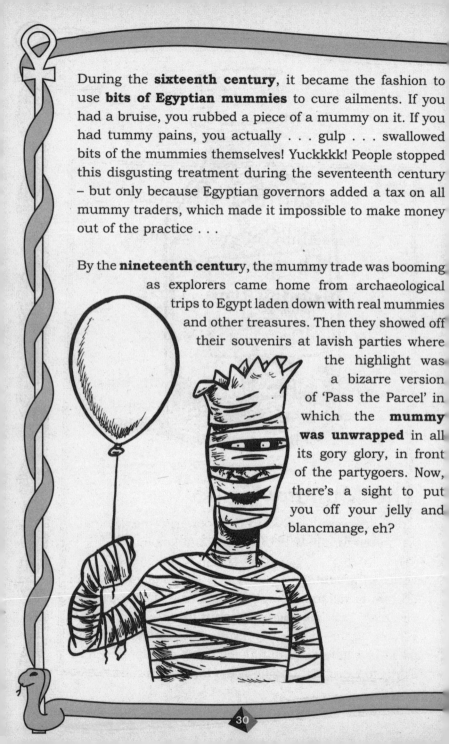

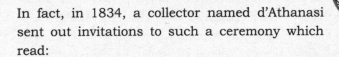

In fact, in 1834, a collector named d'Athanasi sent out invitations to such a ceremony which read:

Giovanni d'Athanasi

respectfully informs the public
that on the evening of

Monday 10th April

next at

5 o'clock,

the most interesting mummy which has
ever been discovered in Egypt
will be unwrapped in the
large room at

Exeter Hall.

Tickets next to the unwrapping table – 6 shillings

Balcony and platform seats – 4 shillings

All other seats in the hall cost
2 shillings and sixpence.

This next story has become popular over the years. Apparently, the **mummy of Princess Amen-Ra** – contained inside an impressive wooden sarcophagus – was bought by an English lord and transported on a ship crossing the Atlantic in **April 1912**. Because it was so special, it was stored behind the captain's bridge, rather than in the baggage hold.

Unfortunately, the ship hit a **huge iceberg** near

Newfoundland on the night of **14 April**, and was split open and sank. A total of 4,190 passengers were drowned, and went down with the ship . . . as did the mummy! Bet you've guessed the name of the ship . . . Yes, it was the *Titanic*.

Can that possibly be true? Probably not . . . but it's a good story, isn't it?

3.
Expanding the Egyptian Empire

The Egyptians were a very advanced civilization and worked hard at expanding their empire. Let's hope you don't have to work as hard as you Find That Fib!

Expansion through Trade

Egypt was the world's first nation-state and so became a magnet for trade. The empire expanded all the way from Nubia to Syria as Egypt's trading influence spread far and wide when official missions set out to find **luxury goods** for a pharaoh and his court. Carrying out many land and sea expeditions, the empire acquired resources such as cedar wood from lands as far away as Byblos, in what we now know as Lebanon. Gold came from Nubia to the south, and sheaves of grain came from the Nile Valley.

Ships would sail up and down the Nile with their cargoes. To get to Egypt, traders sailed round the Arabian peninsula, landing on Egypt's Red Sea coast, or sailed up the Nile from the Mediterranean.

Top Five Fave Luxury Trading Goods

1. Timber (particularly Lebanese cedar wood and African ebony)
2. Precious stones
3. Metals (copper and gold from Nubia and bronze from Syria)
4. Spices
5. Pottery (particularly Minoan ceramics from Crete)

The traders often carried such **huge quantities of gold coins**, packed and sealed in wooden chests, that wooden trading boats were frequently in danger of sinking once they set sail. Worried captains had the permission of pharaohs to open sealed chests and throw up to a third of the gold into the Red Sea in order to ease the weight. This tradition was supposed to ensure safe passage.

It was a good job eBay didn't exist in **Hatshepsut**'s day, or she'd have spent all her time trading on that. As it was, this first female pharaoh **encouraged trade** with her fellow royal – Eti, Queen of Punt. Boat after boat set sail with goods to the land of Punt in East Africa. In return, these wooden craft sailed back loaded to the mast with storage jars, spices, gold, ebony, myrrh, ivory, plants, pet apes and greyhounds for Queen Hatshepsut. But Hatshepsut's most famous trade items were **two frankincense trees** from Punt – the first time ever that live trees had been exported anywhere.

In **2240 BC**, provincial governor **Harkhuf** returned from a raiding trip to the southern region of Yam. He was headed for Memphis to give up his booty to the pharaoh, Pepi II. Harkhuf brought with him 300 donkeys carrying packs of elephant tusks, leopard skins, incense and ebony. The gift that most pleased the pharaoh was a **captured pygmy**! Mind you, Pharaoh Pepi was only eight years old.

Work in Ancient Egypt

Quickie Quiz

During the busy harvest season, *workers* toiled for many hours in the fields. How were they paid? Was it:

a) only when they asked?
b) payment in grain?
c) once in a blue moon?

*The answer's **b)**. They were paid – but not in cash. Payment was generally as much grain as a worker could gather together during one day in the fields.*

Thanks to their skill at mummifying bodies, Egyptian **doctors** knew a lot about broken bones and surgery. However, they still believed in **magic powers** to help them heal people. To make sure that treatment would succeed, they used all sorts of potions, amulet charms, and ancient spells to keep disease at bay. Turn to page 44 for more medical marvels.

Butchers in Egyptian times wore **platform shoes** to do their work! Butchers' work sandals were made with a slice of cork sandwiched between two layers of leather. Three pieces of sole were held together by small wooden pegs. This gave them an extra 30 centimetres in height, so that they could stand above a chopping area as they hacked away at bones and flesh.

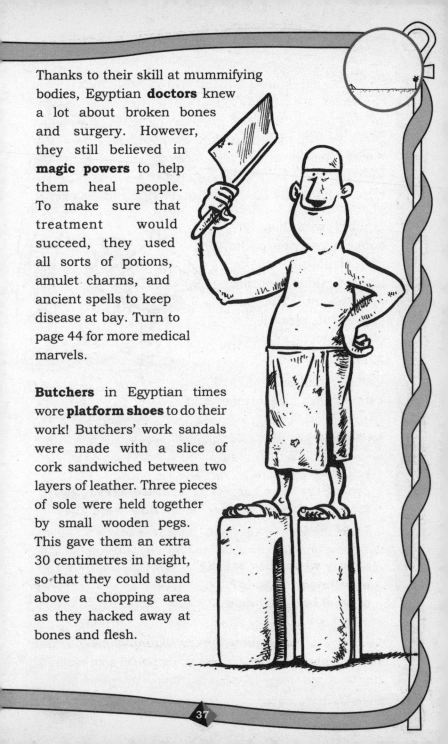

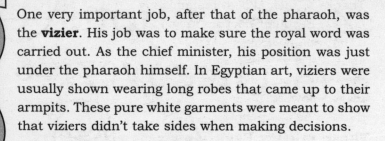

One very important job, after that of the pharaoh, was the **vizier**. His job was to make sure the royal word was carried out. As the chief minister, his position was just under the pharaoh himself. In Egyptian art, viziers were usually shown wearing long robes that came up to their armpits. These pure white garments were meant to show that viziers didn't take sides when making decisions.

A very popular job in ancient Egypt was to be a **priest**, as there were thousands of them. Individual priests were members of a team which worked round the clock, dividing up hours of the day or night into watches. Their duties included performing ceremonies at shrines and temples, organizing week-long festivals in praise of their many gods and producing passion plays in honour of the great god Osiris.

Archaeologists digging near the pyramids of Giza and Saqqara found a cemetery containing 600 tombs. They were the graves of the ordinary **workers** who built the pyramids, and their skeletons showed what a tough job it was. Many had squashed backbones, as a result of carrying heavy loads. Some were even missing fingers and legs. A few of these graves were also covered with mini-pyramids several metres high.

4. Inventions and Discoveries

Those mighty Egyptians were also mighty clever when it came to inventing things. Now it's your chance to show how clever you can be when it comes to Finding That Fib!

The 'papyrus' is a rather useful reed that grows on the banks of the Nile. The Egyptians peeled off the outer layers, then cut the pith inside the reed into strips.

Once they'd taken the pith and soaked it in water, the Egyptians criss-crossed strips and hammered them until they were squashed flat. The sheet was smoothed out with a piece of wood, and it resulted in **papyrus paper**!

Ancient pictures have led historians to believe that the **plough** was invented by Egyptians. Paintings on tomb walls show a bow-shaped stick being dragged across the ground.

The Nile was a vital part of getting around the Egyptian empire. That's probably why the Egyptians invented the world's first **inflatable rafts**. They carefully sewed two large linen squares together, and sealed the edges with candle grease. They then used a reed to inflate the raft and . . . hey presto! Instant river transport!

A piece of papyrus found in **850 BC** was covered in **mathematical calculations** for working out the areas of squares, triangles and circles.

Builders and engineers would use these to find out land areas, heights of buildings, and how much grain could be stored in places.

A **Nilometer** was a handy device for measuring how deep the River Nile was at any time. It was simply a series of steps on the river bank. Farmers would need a flood of 7 metres to irrigate their land for crops. Less floodwater would dry out the fields, and more would destroy buildings and drainage channels.

Ancient Egyptian women invented the first **hair gel**. They used to slap a concoction of soil and water on their hair after having wrapped it round primitive curlers made of wood. Then they'd bask under the desert sun to keep their hair in place.

Quickie Quiz
How did Egyptians *measure* things?
Did they use:

a) calculators made of wood?
b) units of measurement called cubits?
c) a lot of guesswork?

*The answers **b**. Egyptians used a unit of measurement called a cubit, which was the length of a man's forearm. That length was then subdivided into palms and fingers . . . which, if you didn't have a ruler, came in handy! A royal cubit was 52 centimetres in length, and a short cubit was 45 centimetres.*

41

The Egyptians were responsible for **domesticating the modern cat** and, in fact, most cats today are descended from Egyptian cats. Farmers tamed them and kept them as pets, training them to catch mice and protect their grain stores. The Egyptian word for cat was 'miw', which means 'to see', and it sounds like our modern 'mew' or 'miaow'.

The ancient Egyptians invented a simple **water clock** that allowed water to escape through a hole in the bottom of a bowl. A fall in the water level meant that they could see marks on the side which corresponded to the hours. Water leaked through at the rate of about ten drops per second and the sides of the bowl were angled to make sure that water flowed steadily, no matter how much was left inside.

We can't actually tell whether **sandals** were invented by the Egyptians . . . but they certainly wore them! Originally, sandals were made from a footprint in wet sand. Braided papyrus reed was then moulded into the imprint to form soles. Sandals were held in place on the foot by palm-fibre thongs, which passed between the toes. Once the Egyptians learned to tan hide, sandals were made with a leather sole.

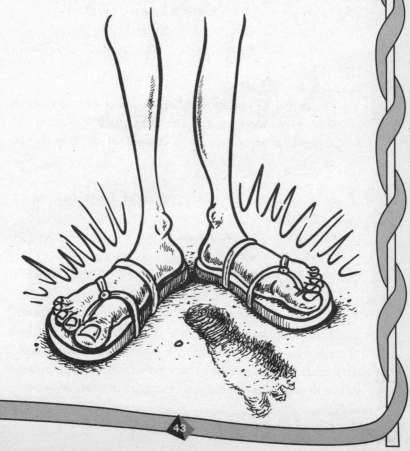

Medical Marvels

Doctors in Egyptian times concocted **medical potions** that contained fairly disgusting ingredients. The dung (or poo) of various animals, fat from cats, fly droppings and even whole cooked mice were some of the ingredients that ancient medics recommended patients swallow to make themselves better.

Two Ways to Cure a Headache, Egyptian-Style

1. Inhale the smoke from burning sandals.

2. Take a mixture of the following: juniper berries, wormwood, coriander and honey. Squash them into a paste and rub them on your scalp.

Quickie Quiz

What did Egyptian doctors prescribe to patients who were suffering from that most common of Egyptian ailments, eye infections? Was it to drink:

a) **40 gallons of water straight from the River Nile?**

b) **bat blood, tortoise gall bladder, and dried liver of a swallow?**

c) **a diet version of cola made from grapes, sulphur and pig fat?**

The answer's b). It seems that swigging back a glass of bat blood, tortoise gall bladder and dried liver of a swallow did the trick!

How to Cure Baldness (around 1500 BC)

1. Recite magic spell to Sun god

2. Swallow mixture of:

Onions

Honey

Red Lead

Iron

Alabaster

And presto! Your hair should stay in place.

Around 400 years later, huge advances in hair treatment had obviously been made:

How to Cure Baldness (around 1100 BC)

Rub potion on to scalp consisting of fat from:

Lions

Crocodiles

Ibex (a mountain goat)

Serpents

Geese

Hippopotami

Or if these methods fail, rubbing some **chopped lettuce** leaves on your bald patch would supposedly encourage hair growth.

5. Fashion

With all those pyramids to build, you wouldn't think that the ancient Egyptians would worry much about how they looked. However, it turns out they were a very fashionable race. So read on . . . and don't forget to Find That Fib!

Hair Trends

Over the years, Egyptian women liked to change their hairstyles. Women in the Old Kingdom preferred to have short cuts or chin-length bobs. However, in the New Kingdom, women kept their hair long or even wore wigs. The men, however, kept their hair neat, short and above their ears.

Women decorated their hair with linen ribbons to keep lotus blossoms in place. In time, these were replaced by coronets or diadems made of gold, garnet, malachite and turquoise beads. Poorer people used simpler and cheaper ornaments of petals and berries.

The **children** of ancient Egypt had rather strange hairstyles. Their hair was shaved off or cut short except for a long, **dangling lock** of hair left on the side of the head. This was known as the 'side-lock of youth' and often fell in an s-shape, which is probably why an s-shaped lock is also the hieroglyphic symbol for a child. Boys and girls wore this style until the onset of puberty.

Then, young boys often shaved their entire heads, while young girls grew and plaited their hair or wore it in a ponytail style, hanging down the centre of their back. Young girl dancers wore long, thick, braided ponytails, weighted down at the ends with beads or metal discs.

Some Egyptian men and women **shaved** their hair off so that they were more comfortable in the hot climate, and kept free of troublesome head lice. However, it wasn't the done thing for women especially to be seen with a bald head, and so they wore **wigs** made from human hair, sheep's wool or vegetable fibre.

Slaves and **servants** wore their hair differently from noble men and women. They often **looped** their hair up at the back of the head. Another variation was to tie it in eight or nine **long plaits** at the back of the head and then pull them together, over one side of the neck or face.

Quickie Quiz
At banquets, as they enjoyed their meals, what did ancient Egyptians of noble birth wear to look extremely trendy? Was it:

a) a pair of linen shorts?
b) a hoodie?
c) blobs of grease on their hair?

The answer's c). Pictures dating from Egyptian times show diners wearing a cone-like blob of perfumed grease on their heads. I bet you're wondering why – but no one really knows.
Some historians think it was so that the grease would melt in the heat, and release a lovely perfumed smell. Others wonder whether it was drawn in by artists who wanted to point out that the grease-coned dinner guests were actually wearing false hairpieces or wigs that were scented!

Egyptian Clothing

Wool was almost unknown as a fabric in ancient Egypt – it would've been too hot to wear in the desert, anyway. Silk and cotton were brought by foreign rulers and became popular after about 1000 BC.

Egyptian **men** usually wore a **simple tunic**, **kilt** or **loin cloth**. However, a type of shirt was found in the tomb of Tarkhan, which was made 5,000 years ago.

Egyptian **women** wore a **long dress** that fitted their bodies closely. From the Middle Kingdom onwards, pleats, straps and folds were incorporated to make the outfits look more stylish, as did adding beads and feathers as decoration.

Quickie Quiz

What did Egyptian women and men grow to love wearing? Was it:

a) **wide colourful collars?**
b) **T-shirts made of woven reed stalks and mud?**
c) **pre-stressed, ripped, and gold-threaded tunics?**

It's a). Women and men wore wide, decorated collars that were made of glass beads, berries, leaves and flowers.

Stylish Pharaohs

You could always spot a pharaoh from a mile off! He'd be the one with a **1-metre-long beard** which trailed over his shoulder and was held off the ground by a '**beard bearer**', a young nine-year-old boy. Ribbons woven into the beard made it seem longer than it actually was. Jewelled medallions – made from amethyst and turquoise – were also woven into the pharaoh's beard, to show his royal status.

The **double crown** that was worn by the pharaohs was called the *pschent*. It was a tall, cone-like headdress, symbolizing the bringing together (or unification) of the two Egyptian kingdoms.

The white part, or *hedjet*, at the top of the *pschent* was a symbol of **Upper Egypt**.

The *deshret* – which represents **Lower Egypt** – is the red section at the bottom of the *pschent*.

Footwear indicated how powerful or influential you were in Egyptian society and, naturally, the pharaoh's shoes were the most lavish.

In 3000 BC, a barefoot slave was shown carrying

Pharaoh Narmer's sandals, which indicates that sandals were probably only worn by royalty, to protect royal feet from burning sands.

But by about 1552 BC, **Queen Hatshepsut** was thought to have made sandals trendy. She is said to have worn jewel-covered sandals and enjoyed bathing her feet in scented oil.

The mummy of **King Tutankhamun** had embossed gold sandals with pointed toes curled upwards. The sandals were provided for the deceased to walk around in comfort in the afterlife.

Make Me Beautiful

You've probably seen pictures of Egyptian women with heavy black lines round their eyes. This make-up was called *kohl* and it was made from pounding a **lead-based** mineral called *galena* to powder, and then mixing it with water. At least it was used . . . until people discovered that the lead was poisonous! Thereafter, Egyptian women played it safe and made up their eyes with **soot** instead. In the early period, green eye make-up was also popular.

The Four Steps to an Egyptian Woman's Toilette

1. Use a finger or a special wooden instrument to apply kohl round the eyes.
2. Colour in lips and cheeks with red ochre.
3. Paint henna on to the soles of feet and on to fingernails to turn them a trendy red colour.
4. Dye any pesky grey hairs with henna.

Men and women also used **combs**, **tweezers**, **shavers** and **hair curlers** to keep themselves looking neat and tidy.

Egyptian men used to **shave** with a stone blade at first, later with a copper, and during the Middle Kingdom with a bronze razor.

6.
Superstitious Traditions

In ancient Egypt, rituals (however silly they seem now) were of the utmost importance in bringing wealth and prosperity. Good luck to you as you try to Find That Fib among the following facts.

Scarab beetles were believed to be very sacred in Egyptian times. People dipped stone or pottery scarabs into wax and used them as seals for letters. Or they made models of these chunky insects for ring decorations or lucky charms.

Egyptians often wore charm bracelets with pictures of eyes on them. This represented the eye of Horus, the falcon-god, and was known as an *udjat* eye, protecting those who wore it. Necklaces or earrings also featured *udjat* charms to prevent misfortune.

Bes was a god represented as an ugly bearded dwarf dressed in a leopard-skin thong and wearing an ostrich feather on his head. (Hey, Bes . . . nice look!) With style like that, you'd probably wonder why Egyptians risked nightmares by carving the monstrous image of Bes on to their bedheads. That's because he was considered to be the **guardian of sleep**, who chased away evil spirits and guaranteed sweet dreams.

Despite having fallen out of the ugly tree, and having hit every branch on the way down, statues of Bes could be seen in Egyptian houses on little pillars covered with magic formulae. This representation of the god Bes **protected the whole family** against nasty beasts such as crocodiles, snakes, lions or scorpions.

Priests traditionally shaved off all their body hair – including their eyebrows and eyelashes – performing this ritual every third day. This was to prevent them being troubled by head lice, and to ensure they were **scrupulously clean** to perform religious rituals.

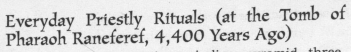

Everyday Priestly Rituals (at the Tomb of Pharaoh Raneferef, 4,400 Years Ago)

1. Lead daily procession, circling pyramid three times.
2. Pull covering from statue of Raneferef.
3. Sprinkle statue with perfume.

4. Paint black eyeshadow on statue.
5. Wave incense burner under statue's nose.
6. Dress it again in bright-coloured cloths.
7. Don't forget to chant secret formulae while doing all of the above!
8. Supervise line of bread-bearers, as they leave offerings on altar.

This huge **mountain of bread offerings** would be left on the altar for an hour before being removed. During that time, it was thought that **Raneferef**'s 'Ka' or 'spirit' was received and nourished by the bread.

Egyptian priests also spent time **studying the stars**. They thought that the planets were gods, and called Sirius, the brightest star in the sky, 'Sopdet' after a goddess. This star rose in the sky at a time when everyone was waiting for the Nile to flood, so – in thanks – the star was celebrated by a special festival.

Worshipping Animals

If you were born the right kind of animal in ancient Egypt, you were dead lucky as you were worshipped and even led a life of luxury in the temples.

Cats were at the top of the worship scale. If a temple caught fire in ancient Egypt, Egyptians would dash into the burning building – with no thought for their own safety – in an attempt to rescue any fire-singed felines. In fact, cats were so revered that if you killed one, either by accident or on purpose, you were **put to**

death immediately without trial. A visiting Greek historian, Diodorus, described a god-fearing mob setting upon a Roman who had killed a cat during the reign of Ptolemy Auletes. Though everyone knew that the kitty's death had been accidental, the angry Egyptians made sure that the clumsy cat-killer never struck again!

Wars sometimes broke out between tribes when a **sacred animal** from one locality was found to have been . . . errr . . . **killed** by another clan's hunters! During the first century of the Christian era, the Romans had to step in and end a war between two Egyptian tribes. How did that war begin? Well, it seems

that the Oxyrhynchites worshipped a **spider crab** and the Cynopolitans worshipped a **dog**. Now, when the Cynopolitans thoughtlessly ate a crab, the other lot killed and ate the dogs of their enemies in a bloodthirsty revenge attack.

When sacred animals did die, then it was very important to give the deceased creature a **lavish funeral**. Hundreds of thousands of reptiles, birds, animals and fish of all species have been found in cemeteries all over Egypt. In **Beni Hasan**, for example, so many cats have been found in the cemetery, the remains were made into **fertilizer**. Also, huge cemeteries filled with mummified **Nile Valley crocodiles** have been discovered, along with baby crocs and their eggs.

When the **sacred Apis bull died** after a lifetime being tended and worshipped, the pharaoh himself dropped all royal duties to take charge of the funeral. After all, the sacred bull was the **reincarnation of Ptah**, Egypt's third most popular god, and was given a fittingly splendid send-off.

The Apis bull's temple at the ancient Egyptian capital city of Memphis was built to honour the great miracles performed by the god Ptah. One of these was the time when Ptah saved Pelusium from an attack by Assyrian soldiers. Ptah had the bright idea of getting together an army of rats to defend the city, and those ranks of rodent renegades forced the Assyrian attackers to back off by nibbling through their quivers, bowstrings and the leather thongs of their shields!

Quickie Quiz

When Ptah was re-born as Bull Apis, only priests could spot which of the following distinguishing features?

a) A white triangle on his forehead
b) A flying vulture on his back
c) A crescent moon on his right side
d) An image of a scarab beetle on his tongue
e) Double hairs on his tail
f) A tattoo of his wife's name on his right leg

a), b), c), d) and e)! Bull Apis had nearly *all* the above distinguishing features – except, obviously, for the tattoo on his left leg!

Ancient Egyptians were known for being extremely hard-working. However, if anyone was accused of laziness – either by fellow-workers or bosses – they were immediately sent to the Temple of Bahd Jokhe, and told to pray to **Bennu**, the **sacred slug**. This slow-moving mollusc looked after the lazy and protected them from being sacked.

Creature Features
Sixteen Animal Heads on Egyptian Gods' Bodies

Name	Type of Animal Head
Amon (or Amun)	Ram with curved horns
Anubis	Jackal
Bast	Cat
Buto	Serpent
Happy	Baboon
Hathor	Cow
Heqet	Frog
Khepri	Scarab Beetle
Nefertum	Lion
Nekhebet	Vulture
Ra-Harakhty	Falcon
Sekhmet	Lioness
Serket	Scorpion (worn on her head)
Seth	Unidentifiable hybrid animal
Taueret	Hippopotamus
Upuaut	Wolf

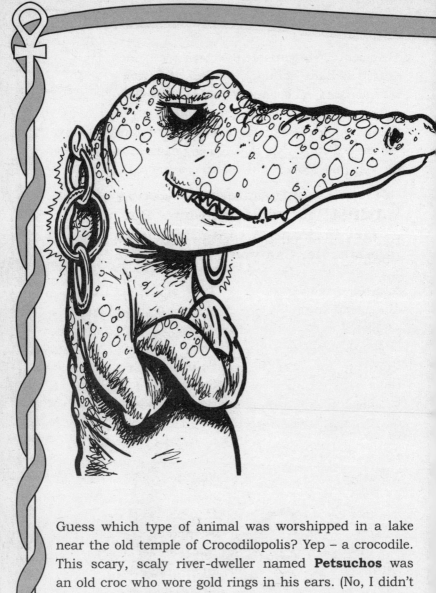

Guess which type of animal was worshipped in a lake near the old temple of Crocodilopolis? Yep – a crocodile. This scary, scaly river-dweller named **Petsuchos** was an old croc who wore gold rings in his ears. (No, I didn't think crocs had ears, either – but who is going to argue with a beast like that?) **Feeding Pete the Croc** became a **great tourist attraction** as priests held open his jaws to feed him cake, roast meat and honey wine.

7. Food and Drink

Here's a mouth-watering selection of titbits to get your teeth into. But don't forget that one of these facts is an out-and-out lie. Can you Find That Fib?

The Egyptians seem to have been **healthy eaters** and enjoyed their five portions of fruit and veg a day. Believe it or not, they loved **boiled cabbage**, and often began their meals with a plate full of the stuff. They also ate large amounts of health-giving **garlic**. Other fruit and veg, home-grown in the household veggie patch, included cucumbers, radishes, leeks, olives, chickpeas, lentils, dates, figs, turnips, beans and grapes.

Menu for Working Egyptians
Bread
Porridge
Salted Fish
Onions
Beer

Menu for Posh Royal Banquet
Roast Goose
Stewed Beef
Kidneys
Wild Duck
Cut of Gazelle
Served with:
Leeks, stewed with milk and cheese
Choice of red or white wine

***

For Dessert:
**Dates, grapes, pomegranates, melons,
peaches, pears, cherries**

Chef
Do **not** . . . repeat **not** . . . cook lamb
or fish at tonight's royal banquet.
Some guests are **very** religious, and
all hell could break loose if such
items were on the menu!

Ptolemy

Bread was baked in really big loaves during Egyptian times. This was so that one loaf could feed a lot of people. Bread was the most common food in Old Egypt, and symbolized wealth and abundance.

Bread was also an important ingredient in **making beer**. The god Osiris was said to have brought beer to Egypt, well over 3,000 years ago. To make this sweet, grainy brew, workers had to squish some barley bread in water and add some hops. That mixture fermented and turned to alcohol, before being strained off into a tub made of wood.

Egyptians also enjoyed **sarnies** and **butties**. They hollowed out the centre of the thick loaves and filled them with beans, vegetables or other items. They also made a flat bread with raised edges so that it could hold eggs, or other fillings.

Flour used to make bread was very gritty. Perhaps pieces of quartz or felspar – mineral fragments broken off from utensils used to mix the flour – contributed to the flour's grittiness. In fact, many mummies have been discovered with teeth that have been ground right down after a lifetime of eating Egyptian bread.

Pastry chefs baked fancy cakes in all sorts of shapes, ranging from ring doughnuts to pyramids, and from spirals to cakes shaped like crocodiles. They were sweetened with honey rather than sugar.

Wines – both red and white – were made from grapes taken from vineyards, pressed and stored in pottery jars rather than bottles, which were then marked with the year . . . just like the label on a modern-day bottle of wine.

If a **vegetarian** sat down to a meal in ancient Egypt, it was thought by your hosts to be insulting if you did not smear a small circle of cottage cheese or yoghurt in the middle of your forehead. It served as a message to the chef, who then didn't serve you any meat.

Quickie Quiz
What did Egyptians do with freshly killed meat? Did they:

a) **eat it quickly?**
b) **put it in a refrigerator?**
c) **preserve it through salting, drying or smoking?**

The answer's c). Sometimes, however, beer, honey or fish eggs were used to help preserve meat that would go off quickly in the searing heat.

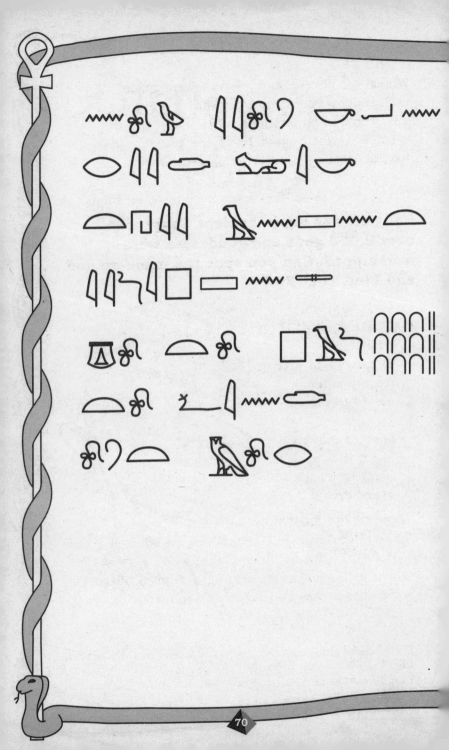

8. Egyptian Gods

Religion was big in ancient Egypt and over 2,000 gods and goddesses were worshipped. Can you spot the made-up god and Find That Fib?

Early Egyptian Gods

Tribes started worshipping their animal gods as far back as the early settlements in 6000 BC. After 3,000 years those animal gods started to be thought of as having human form . . . while bits of the animal were left behind.

You end up with gods in human form, but with an animal head. Or, at the very least, with little animal horns or ears.

Some of the most popular gods

Amon (sometimes spelt 'Amun') was the name of a great deity also known as 'King of the Gods'. He was often shown in human form, wearing a plumed headdress. Sometimes he was also shown as a human with a ram's head.

The god **Anubis**, represented as a jackal or dog-headed god, was the god of death. He was known as 'Lord of the Land', which meant that he was in charge of the cemetery. Another nickname was 'Lord of the Mummy Wrappings' because he bound up the mummy of Osiris to stop his body from decomposing. Painted around 1200 BC, you can see Anubis doing his mummification in a tomb painting at Deir el Medina.

Anubis was always present at funerals, taking the hand of the dead and leading them before the sovereign judges for the weighing of souls. He also had to make sure that any offerings brought by the dead person's family actually reached their recently departed!

The cat-goddess **Bast** (or Bastet in her pure cat form) loved pleasure and music and became really popular in the fourth century BC. Every year, an annual festival was held at her temple in Bubastis. Thousands journeyed by barge, from all over Egypt, for a party to the sound of flutes and castanets. It was a day for drinking wine in huge quantities (more on that day than at any other time of the year), and also for burying mummified bodies of cats.

Horus, the falcon god, was considered to be the most important divine being from the very earliest of times. Many Egyptians thought of the sky as a divine falcon whose two eyes were the Sun and the Moon. Horus was the son of Isis and Osiris and was shown as a falcon or falcon-headed god.

Worshipping the falcon was so popular that there were, rather confusingly, twenty gods dedicated to the bird. For example, the god **Harpokrates** was 'the infant Horus'. In ancient drawings, he was shown wearing a rather strange top hat, with a pair of wings flapping from the sides, which allowed the young lad to hover several metres above the ground.

Geb was the Earth god. He's depicted as a normal enough man, but sometimes has a goose on his head! Geb's described in certain legends as a gander – also known as 'The Great Cackler' – whose female mate has laid the Sun, in egg form. Geb was known as 'father of the gods' because he handed over his power as ruler to his eldest son Osiris.

Osiris was one of the most important gods. He was dark-green-skinned, drop-dead gorgeous, and much taller than other men. When dad Geb kicked the bucket, legend has it Osiris became Egypt's first pharaoh. On his death, he became ruler of the Underworld.

An Ancient Post-it Note: Things To Do Now I Am Pharaoh (by Osiris)

1. Make Isis, my sister, my queen.

2. Knowing that early Egyptians had horrible habits, stop them eating one another! (The thought of my subjects being cannibals leaves a nasty taste in the mouth . . .)

3. Teach my subjects to become farmers and grow grain and grapes in order to make wine, bread and beer.

4. Civilize the people of Egypt, by making them build towns and by giving them laws that are just.

5. Build temples, create first divine images, and start cult of gods.

6. Civilize nations outside Egypt, by using combination of gentleness, song and playing various musical instruments.

Ra was the great Sun god, sovereign lord of the sky whom the Egyptians worshipped as creator of the world. All living things, including humans, were said to have sprung from Ra's tears. That might be because the word 'tears' and the word 'men' apparently both sound the same in the Egyptian language!

Top Four Ways in which Ra has been Drawn by Ancient Egyptians

1. As a royal child, at rest on the lotus bud that had given birth to him.

2. As a man with a ram's head.

3. As a man with a falcon's head.

4. As a man with a head surrounded by a flaming disc and a fire-spitting asp called an *uraeus*.

Sekhmet was the lioness god of war who attacked Sun-god Ra's enemies so ferociously that poor Ra feared for the safety of the entire human race! He begged her to stop, but Sekhmet simply said, 'When I slay men, my heart rejoices.'

That's when Ra came up with a cunning plan – he mixed up several thousand jugs of a magic potion of beer and pomegranate juice. Thirsty Sekhmet drank these on the battlefield, mistaking the liquid for human blood. She became so drunk, she couldn't carry on killing any more humans.

Seth was Osiris's violent **brother**, who was so jealous of his achievements that he plotted against him and killed him. When Osiris's faithful wife, **Isis**, heard about this, she went bonkers! She cut off her hair, tore her robes, and tracked down the coffin containing her dead hubbie Osiris, which had been thrown into the Nile.

Using sorcery, and with the help of Thoth, Anubis and Horus, Isis brought Osiris's battered body back to life.

Seth finally became the spirit of evil, in eternal opposition to the spirit of good.

We should've guessed that Seth would be a 'bad 'un' – he was born by tearing himself violently from his mother's womb. He also had unusually white skin and bright red hair, which is probably why, traditionally, Egyptians mistrusted redheads!

Thoth – Different Ways in which he was Represented

An ibis

A man with an ibis's head

A dog-headed ape

A baboon

Quickie Quiz

Apart from acting as Moon-god, what sort of jobs did *Thoth do*? Did he:

a) have to encourage use of science, literature, wisdom and inventions?

b) invent hieroglyphics as a way of writing?

c) act as spokesman of the gods, and keep records?

d) lounge around all day, watching the telly and eating crisps?

d) is the only thing Thoth *didn't* do. He was kept busy with the stuff in answers *a)*, *b)* and *c)* . . .

9.
Pharaohs

The rulers of Egypt were usually men, but a few powerful women were also given the crown . . . which is pharaoh nuff! Now then, can you Find That Fib among this lot?

The pharaoh was often depicted carrying a **crook and flail**, which were symbols of authority. The crook (a bendy hook used by shepherds to rescue sheep) was a symbol of kingship. The flail (a handle and chain used to thresh grain from crops) symbolized the fertile land.

Supposedly, the god Osiris used to enjoy carrying around crooks 'n' flails which is why these soon became known as badges of royal office.

Khafra (Reigned 2558–2532 BC)
As son of Pharaoh Khufu, Khafra built the Great Pyramid in Giza, which is guarded by the great Sphinx.

Hatshepsut (Reigned 1498–1483 BC)
Female ruler Hatshepsut was wife of Thutmose II and also his half-sister. She wore the male traditional dress of the pharaoh and reigned successfully for fifteen years, building many monuments and temples.

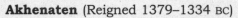

Akhenaten (Reigned 1379–1334 BC)

When Akhenaten came to the ancient Egyptian throne, he brought with him a change in belief. Previously the Egyptian people had believed in many gods. Under Akhenaten, they were told to worship only the Sun god Aten.

Not only that, but Akhenaten moved the capital from Memphis to a place he modestly named Akhenaten! People probably forgave him because his wife – Queen Nefertiti – was so beautiful.

Tutankhamun
(Reigned 1334–1325 BC)

The most famous pharaoh of them all came to the Egyptian throne when he was only nine years old. He died at the age of eighteen – and was buried among amazing treasures in a tomb in the Valley of the Kings.

Istantaten (Reigned 1324 BC)
The most powerful female pharaoh of all, Istantaten defeated the Persians in battle and declared war on the Nubians. During her reign Egypt was established as a great military nation, and her battle tactics became famous.

She reigned for a year before her early death – not on the battlefield but from her eye make-up! The kohl she used contained lead, which poisoned her. After this, Egyptian women stopped using kohl.

Horemheb (Reigned 1323 BC)
Horemheb didn't get to become pharaoh through royal birth. He was a nobleman who became a brilliant military commander, making his move to grab the throne at the end of the eighteenth dynasty, building on his experience as deputy and prince regent of Tutankhamun.

Rameses II (Reigned 1279–1212 BC)

The son of Seti I, Rameses built many beautiful temples, and had Nefertari as his chief queen. Rameses defied the odds by living to the fine old age of ninety-two, had 200 wives and concubines, and had twenty sons and twenty daughters.

Cleopatra VII (Reigned 51–30 BC)

Coming to the throne at the age of eighteen as co-ruler with her brother, Cleopatra was the last of the Ptolemaic rulers of Egypt, and lover of Roman leaders Julius Caesar and Mark Antony. Centuries later, she was also the subject of several plays (including Shakepeare's *Antony and Cleopatra*) and various films. Legend has it that she killed herself with a poisonous snake – probably an Egyptian cobra, which was also known as an asp.

10. Pyramids and Tombs

But how much do you know about these amazing monuments? Test your knowledge as you Find That Fib!

The mighty, magical, majestic pyramids of ancient Egypt – built to help a pharaoh live forever – drew resources from all over the kingdom and beyond. Farmers were forced into national service to feed workers during their construction.

Within each pyramid was a **stash of fantastic treasure**, left there for the pharaoh to enjoy in the next life. Items included golden furniture encrusted with precious stones, and equally expensive chariots, royal clothing, weapons, jewels and boxes of food.

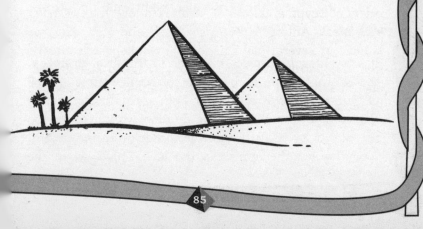

The First Pyramid, 2630 BC

The **Step Pyramid**, built to honour Pharaoh Djoser, was Egypt's first pyramid. It was built at Saqqara (aka Sakkara), around 2630 BC close to the capital city of Memphis. The Step Pyramid represented a ladder, by which the soul of the dead ruler might walk up into the sky to join the gods.

It was a massive project, overseen by the vizier **Imhotep**, the pharaoh's first minister. He assembled three groups of workers. He arranged for one workforce to quarry limestone at the cliff of Tura, another workforce to ship the blocks by boat up the Nile to Saqqara, and a third team hauled the stones to the site. That's when the blocks of granite – some weighing as much as 72,000 kilograms each – were shaped by master carvers and put in place on the pyramid.

Some people think that the Egyptians couldn't possibly have built the pyramids, but instead, aliens were responsible. So, here are a few reasons:

Why Some People Think Egyptian Pyramids were Built by Aliens

1. Pyramids are huge buildings, built to precise calculations thousands of years ago. The ancient Egyptians were simple people so the pyramids must've been built by more intelligent beings . . . namely, aliens!

2. A 47-metre-long passage leads to one of the three burial chambers but no pharaoh's body has ever been found inside the Great Pyramid. So, that must mean the pyramid was built for some other mysterious purpose known only to . . . aliens!

3. The Egyptians normally kept complete records of all their work. However, no records have ever been found for the construction of the Great Pyramid. That must mean it was built by someone *other* than the Egyptians, such as . . . aliens!

4. From up in the skies, if you look down on all the pyramids of Egypt, they seem to be in the exact same position as the formation of stars in Orion's Belt. Perhaps they were meant to form a signal to fellow aliens?

Unless you are able to actually ask an alien why they built the pyramids, it is a pretty safe bet to believe that the pyramids were built by thousands of sweating, muscle-straining **Egyptian labourers**, on the orders of early engineers, mathematicians and all-round clever dicks who combined their knowledge to create these spectacular monuments to their pharaohs.

Great Pyramid at Giza Fact File

- It was built for the Pharaoh Khufu, upon his death in 2566 BC.
- Lying in the pharaoh's chamber, Khufu's body was protected by the pyramid while he journeyed to meet the gods after having died.
- Until the nineteenth century, it was the largest building in the world (at 137 metres, it's twice as high as the Statue of Liberty).
- Its base is 230m square, and its tip used to be 147m high.
- It's made up of around two and a half million stone blocks.
- Each block weighs 2.5 tonnes.
- Outer blocks were covered in bright white limestone (this has now gone).
- It took almost twenty-five years to lay the millions of tonnes of rock in place.
- The capstone at the peak of the pyramid was probably gold-covered.
- It was built by around 10,000 men (far fewer than the earlier estimate of 100,000 men).

The Sphinx and its Nose

The mysterious Sphinx that guards the three pyramids at Giza is a massive stone statue of a lion with a man's head. It may well be the face of Pharaoh Khafra. Most Egyptologists believe that the Sphinx was built in 2500 BC.

Looking east, towards the rising sun, for nearly 4,500 years it was covered in sand blown in from the desert. However, around 1419 BC, Prince Thutmose IV fell asleep between the paws of the Sphinx, and the Sun god Ra appeared and spoke to him. If the prince cleared away the sand, then he was promised he'd be made pharaoh. He did, and he was!

Quickie Quiz

We all know the Sphinx has no nose. How did it lose its hooter? Was it:

a) **blown off by Napoleon, who allowed his troops to use it for target practice?**
b) **blown off by German troops during the First World War?**
c) **blown off in the Second World War by British troops looking for target practice?**

Well, none of those explanations ever happened! So, just what did happen to the Sphinx's nose? An Egyptian historian called al-Maqrizi reckoned that the damage may have occurred around AD 1378 when angry warrior Sa'im al-Dahr objected to peasants making offerings to the Sphinx to increase their harvest, and so destroyed the nose.

It is more likely that due to the harsh desert conditions, it eroded over time. But we do know that sketches drawn in 1737 show the Sphinx's nose was missing even then.

Pyramids naturally attracted the attention of thieves and most were **plundered** by robbers, who were tempted by the vast riches concealed within the burial chambers. After the pharaohs cottoned on to this, they ordered secret, underground burial chambers to be hollowed out into the cliffs on the west bank of the River Nile. This site near Thebes became known as the Valley of the Kings, and was patrolled by guards. Nearby, the Valley of the Queens and Valley of the Nobles were also established.

The Curse of King Tut

Death Shall Come On Swift Wings To Him Who
Disturbs The Peace Of The King.

*These were the words supposedly written on King
Tutankhamun's tomb.*

In 1891 a young Englishman named **Howard Carter**
arrived in Egypt. Newspapers of the day talked of Howard
Carter as a most brilliant man. He was an expert at oil
painting – using actual engine oil – and was a famous
architect, having designed London's Tower Bridge.

But Carter was convinced that there was at least one undiscovered tomb in the **Valley of the Kings** – the tomb belonging to King Tutankhamun. The wealthy **Lord Carnarvon** put up the money to fund the search. Carter dug for five years, but he found no trace of the missing pharaoh.

In **1922**, rising costs made His Lordship call Carter back to England, so that he could tell him he was calling off the search. Carter talked Lord C. into supporting him for one more season of digging.

Carter returned to Egypt with a yellow canary, which his excited foreman felt sure would lead them to the tomb. Maybe it did, as soon after, Carter's workmen uncovered the steps to the tomb. That night, however, Carter returned home to be told that his canary had been eaten by a cobra! Carter brushed aside suggestions that the digging expedition was cursed.

The tomb revealed what Carter described as 'wonderful things . . .' – including a stone sarcophagus which contained three gold coffins nested within each other. Inside the final one was the mummy of the nineteen-year-old boy-king, Pharaoh Tutankhamun.

A few months after the tomb's opening, fifty-seven-year-old Lord Carnarvon was taken ill and rushed to Cairo where he died a few days later. Apparently, he died from an infection started by an insect bite. Legend has it that when he died there was a short power failure and all the lights throughout Cairo went out. His son reported that back in England, at the time of Carnarvon's death, the lord's favourite dog howled and suddenly dropped dead. Even more strange, when the mummy of Tutankhamun was unwrapped in 1925, it was found to have a wound on the left cheek – in the exact same position as the insect bite on Carnarvon that led to his death. Is that spooky, or what?

By 1929, eleven people connected with the discovery of the tomb had died early and of unnatural causes. By 1935, newspaper stories had blamed 'The Curse of King Tut' for the death of twenty-one people.

A Disapproving Tut – at the Curse

In 1934, museum director Herbert E. Winlock worked out that:

1. Of the twenty-two people present when the tomb was opened in 1922, only six had died by 1934.
2. Of the twenty-two people present at the opening of the sarcophagus in 1924, only two died in the following ten years.
3. Of the ten people present when the mummy was unwrapped in 1925, all survived until at least 1934.
4. The figures show that no one involved with the 'Curse of King Tut' died any earlier than would have been expected.

Of deaths that did occur, one German scientist claims that a **fungus spore**, thousands of years old, was responsible for any deaths. This mould had grown on mummies over thousands of years, and – if it was inhaled – it could have proved deadly for humans. It's the sort of sudden death that could be blamed on a deadly mummy's curse!

It seems a curse is most powerful in the mind of a person who believes in it. Howard Carter, the man who actually opened the tomb, never believed in the curse and lived to a reasonably old age of sixty-four before dying of natural causes.

11. Egyptian Writing

There's one reason why we know loads about the Egyptians – they wrote about their lives on everything from tombs to obelisks. But can you separate the facts from the fib?

Luckily for us, the Egyptians liked writing and kept extensive records about their lives. But the Egyptians didn't just write on papyrus, they also wrote on the sides of cows. Only the most important messages were scribbled with a reed pen and ink on the side of these sacred beasts, and only priests were allowed by the gods to write those messages. They only wrote very short messages because the cows didn't really enjoy having notes scribbled on them.

The divine Pharaoh rools!

How to Write in Ancient Egypt

1. Take block of charcoal or soot.
2. Add water to it on a special palette.
3. Add gum to the inky mix.
4. Dip reed pen into black ink.
5. Scribble away.

(Note – To make red ink use ochre (a compound of iron) instead of soot!)

A **scribe** – or 'sesh' as Egyptians called them – often had to travel to write down records of things such as materials used in building projects, measurements and the like. They had a portable palette for mixing their cakes of inks, and they had a kind of pencil case – containing reed pens, an inkwell, and a grinder for mixing ink pigments. They used to carry it around in a little briefcase which contained documents and probably a packed lunch as well!

Three Ways in which the Egyptians Wrote Things

Hieroglyphics

Since 3100 BC, Egyptians used little pictures called hieroglyphs to stand for objects, sounds or ideas. There were originally about 1,000 of these symbols and they were based on simple pictures of objects like body parts, boats, or birds. Some symbols stood for complete words such as life or travel, while others represented sounds or letters that were put together to make words. The ancient Greeks coined the word 'hieroglyphics' to mean 'sacred carvings'. The hieroglyphic alphabet is shown at the start of this book.

Can you read this message?

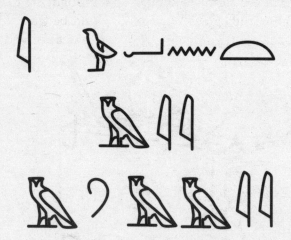

Answer: I want my mummy.

Hieratic Script

A few hundred years later, Egyptians started to transform hieroglyphic symbols into shapes that were more like letters. This speeded up the writing process, and so hieratic was used for stories, business contracts and letters. You had to read messages from right to left.

The message above as it would appear in hieratic script

Demotic Script

This simpler form of writing was brought in towards the end of the Late Period, and it could be written even more quickly than hieratic script. It was also read from right to left.

And again in demotic script.

Demotic script soon took over for business, religious and scientific writing until it died out altogether, when the Romans ruled Egypt.

Quickie Quiz

What was the hieroglyph for a scribe? Was it:

a) a water pot, a brush holder and a palette with cakes of ink?

b) a hippopotamus, wrapped up in red tape?

c) a small, squidgy piece of clay?

The answer is a). Scribes were shown in hieroglyphics as a water pot, a brush holder and a palette with cakes of ink.

The Rosetta Stone

By AD 600, no one understood hieroglyphics any more. Egypt's ancient secrets were lost for 1,200 years . . . until the year 1799. That's when a French soldier discovered a piece of stone at an Egyptian village called el-Rashid or Rosetta.

The Rosetta Stone, as it was called, had the same words written in three different types of writing, representing two languages. Hieroglyphics were at the top, Demotic text in the middle, and Greek at the bottom.

A clever Frenchman named **Jean-François Champollion** did a bit of code-cracking in 1822, and worked out what had been written on the Rosetta Stone by checking the three versions against one another. Working back from the Greek, Champollion realized that the stone contained a royal decree from King Ptolemy V, written in 196 BC. His work led to our modern understanding of Egyptian hieroglyphics.

Use the hieroglyphic alphabet at the beginning of the book to help you complete this ancient Egyptian joke:

What did King Tut write underneath the trumpet hanging outside his tomb?

Hint: read this message downwards, and then left to right.

12. Wars and Battles

Get ready for one last attack on the facts as you Find That Fib!

Egypt wasn't really a warrior nation, but it would defend itself if push came to shove! What worked in Egypt's favour was its geography, as attacking armies didn't have it easy when they set their sights on Egypt. It was surrounded on two sides by desert. It had the Nile cataracts (a series of rapids and waterfalls) in the south and the marshy delta in the north – all of which were barriers to invaders such as the Libyan desert dwellers and Nubian warriors.

Five Neighbouring Nations Who Went to War against Egypt

The Hittites
The Libyans
The Nubians
The Syrians
The Hyksos

Most Egyptians were forced to join an army and, for slaves, enlisting meant they had a chance to gain freedom from slavery once they'd finished their service. Young men from villages learned to drill and prepare for war. In barracks, they were toughened up by a strict regime of physical exercise, wrestling and weapon training. Any breaches of discipline meant that the poor soldiers were thrashed – often by their fellow soldiers.

Brave soldiers were honoured with grants of land, and also given a share of the spoils of the defeated enemy, including slaves. They were also sometimes given trophies with hieroglyphics written on them.

Sometimes, soldiers were given an honour called an *amkhu* to wear. That entitled the bearer to be buried at the expense of the pharaoh.

However, ordinary soldiers didn't get many privileges from fighting wars. If they were lucky, they might get some bread, or wine, or cakes, or meat when the battle was over. Veteran soldiers were given land – but they often had to pay rent upon it.

Quickie Quiz

What were the most prized battle honours given by commanders to their soldiers? Were they:

a) silver models of a sphinx in full battle gear?
b) chain necklaces with dangly bits?
c) cream cakes with jam?

The answer's b). Chain necklaces that had a Golden Fly (or Bee) dangling from them. They were given for bravery.

Queen Ahhotep, mother of Ahmose I, was given three **Golden Flies** for her role in the struggle against the Hyksos – the Canaanite warriors who invaded the Nile Delta around 1650 BC. That award was the Egyptian equivalent of a soldier receiving the Victoria Cross for courage on the battlefield.

Right up until the New Kingdom, Egyptian soldiers didn't bother wearing any armour. They went into battle bare-chested and wearing a short kilt, often wearing a decorative feather in their hair.

Favourite Egyptian Weapons of Warfare

Spears

Shields made of leather or wood

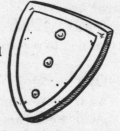

Clubs

Maces

Swords

Daggers

Bows and arrows

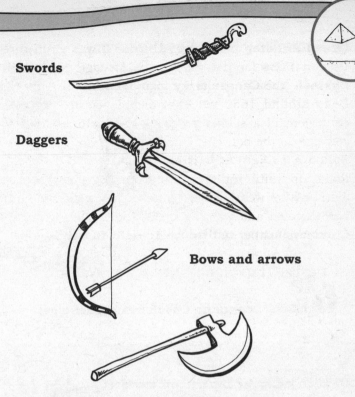

Axes with copper or bronze slicing edges

In 1991, archaeologists uncovered a fleet of fourteen battleships at Abydos, which had been buried beneath the Memphis sands. These boats, dating from 3000 BC, turned out to be the oldest surviving ships in the world and measure up to 30 metres in length!

The Egyptian army was by no means a small affair. Each army division consisted of about 5,000 men, 4,000 of them being infantry troops who were broken down in companies numbering 200 men. The remaining 1,000 men were used in battle as two-man chariot teams.

Different Jobs in the Egyptian Army

Pharaoh (to lead the army into battle)

Soldiers (to fight in battle)

Commanders (to tell troops to fight in battle)

 Scouts (to check out battlefields)

Heralds (to make reports on warfare)

 **Grooms (to care for horses and donkeys that carried baggage)**

Doctors (to care for injured soldiers)

 **Cooks (to feed the troops)**

Spies (to sneak on the enemy)

Scribes (to write up battle reports)

Priests (to make sacrifices to the gods)

Astronomers, astrologers and magicians (to tell superstitious commanders when to strike at the enemy)

Young recruits on training marches were never pushed hard by their officers. They'd only march for a couple of hundred yards a day, and spend the rest of their time playing games like chess, walking on their hands, or holding skipping races to improve their fitness. Juggling fruit was another popular training exercise, aimed at improving hand-to-eye coordination. Skilled soldiers juggled lemons or plums, while less-able recruits tried to catch much bigger fruit like pineapples and grapefruit.

When **Alexander the Great of Greece** fought off the pesky Persian invaders of Egypt, the grateful Egyptians made him a god as well as a pharaoh. When Alex died in 323 BC, his empire was divided up among his three trusty generals.

13. Find That Fib . . . Answers

Chapter 1. Life in Ancient Egypt

I do hope you didn't believe that nonsense about the Nile being divided into 'blue land' and 'pink land'. It was a porkie pie – and if you spotted it, congratulations! You Found The Fib . . .

However, it was completely true that ancient Egyptians thought of Egypt as being divided into two types of land. The only difference was that they referred to the 'black land' and the 'red land'. The 'black land' – rich, black silt left every year after the Nile flooded – was the fertile land used to grow their crops. The 'red land' was the barren desert that protected Egypt on two sides from invading armies.

Chapter 2. Death and Mummification

If you shook your head when you read that a funeral ceremony involved a stilt-walking priest who pelted mourners with mouldy bread, then well done . . . you Found That Fib!

However, it's quite true that priests sprayed milk and other offerings in front of a funeral procession. They also read out spells as people danced in front of a royal tomb.

Chapter 3. Expanding the Egyptian Empire

Did you think there was something fishy when worried captains had the permission of pharaohs to open sealed chests and throw up to a third of the gold into the Red Sea? Well, if you did, you Spotted The Fib!

In reality, Egypt didn't have coinage until the fifth century BC. Instead, goods were exchanged through bartering. Egyptian traders were actually called *shwty* and employed by the Egyptian government.

Chapter 4. Inventions and Discoveries

If you believed that the Egyptians invented the world's first inflatable rafts, then I'm afraid you were caught out! However, the Egyptians did need to sail up and down the Nile, which they did in the time of the Old Kingdom by building boats from papyrus reeds, bound together with string made from reed fibres.

Chapter 5. Fashion

Did you snort in disbelief when you spotted that story about a pharaoh having a 1-metre-long beard, interwoven with ribbons, which trailed over his shoulder? If so, well done – you Found The Fib!

Although Egyptians prided themselves on being clean-shaven, it is true that pharaohs wore false plaited beards which could be attached to a royal wig or crown! Some historians think the custom was meant to remind pharaohs of their heavily bearded ancestors in Africa.

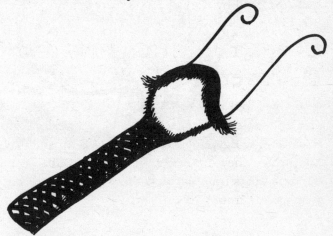

Chapter 6. Superstitious Traditions

If you believed the story about lazy ancient Egyptians avoiding the sack by praying to a sacred slug called Bennu, then I'm afraid you were taken in by the fib! However, there really was a sacred bird called Bennu. Bennu – the bird – was depicted as a lapwing or a heron.

Chapter 7. Food and Drink

If you didn't believe that every time vegetarian Egyptians dined out they had to smear a small circle of yoghurt on their foreheads, then you Found that Fib!

However, ancient Egyptians did realize how important dairy products (like cheese, milk and butter) were. Cattle were raised on land around the delta of the Nile, where the river fans out into the Mediterranean. Those herds also provided meat for Egyptian royalty.

Chapter 8. Egyptian Gods

Remember that tale about the infant Horus – or Harpokrates – wearing a top hat with wings attached, so that the lad could fly a few metres above the ground? Well, if you decided it was untrue, then good on you!

In ancient Egypt, the infant Horus was actually depicted as being a baby with no clothes on, and draped in jewellery. Because this baby god sucked his thumb, he was mistakenly thought by the Greeks to be the god of silence!

Chapter 9. Pharaohs

Did you Spot That Fib? That short reign of warrior Istantaten never happened – because she never existed! In fact, the Egyptians were not likely to declare war on other nations, although they were prepared to defend themselves when necessary.

But it is true that kohl contained lead and that Egyptian women stopped using it when they found it was poisoning them.

Chapter 10. Pyramids and Tombs

If you believed that nonsense about Howard Carter being a genius in all manner of things – like oil painting, writing Shakespeare's plays and so on – then I'm sorry to say you weren't that clever yourself . . . because it was a total untruth! Actually, the opposite is true – archaeologist Howard Carter didn't have much formal education at all. He left school when he was only fifteen, and he used to boast that he never took an exam in his life . . .

Chapter 11. Egyptian Writing

Don't believe that rubbish about Egyptian priests writing messages on the sides of wriggling cows – it was a complete load of tosh!

However, ancient Egyptians actually did write on items other than papyrus – they used fragments of leather, plastered boards and broken pieces of pottery known as *ostraka*.

Chapter 12. Wars and Battles

If you thought that young soldiers not being pushed hard while training was a load of rubbish, then, well done – you Found That Final Fib!

In actual fact, the opposite was true – young soldiers had to undergo tough training because in battle they'd march for up to 19 kilometres a day across burning hot desert regions. They even had their own version of the SAS called 'The Braves'.